PEOPLE & PLACES

Central America

Written by

Marion Morrison

Consultant Jane Peirson Jones

Illustrated by

Ann Savage

SILVER BURDETT PRESS
ENGLEWOOD CLIFFS, NEW JERSEY

U.S. Project Editor Nancy Furstinger
U.S. Editor Ruth Marsh
Editor Caroline White
Designer Robert Mathias, Publishing Workshop
Photo-researcher Hugh Olliff

A TEMPLAR BOOK

Devised and produced by Templar Publishing Co. Ltd.
Pippbrook Mill, London Road, Dorking, Surrey RH4 1JE

Adapted and first published in the United States in 1989
by Silver Burdett Press, Englewood Cliffs, N.J.

Copyright © 1989 by Templar Publishing Co. Ltd.
Illustrations copyright © 1989 by Templar Publishing Co. Ltd.
This adaptation © 1989 by Silver Burdett Press

Color separations by Positive Colour Ltd, Maldon, Essex
Printed by L.E.G.O., Vicenza, Italy

Library of Congress Cataloging-in-Publication Data

Morrison, Marion.
    Central America / written by Marion Morrison;
illustrated by Ann Savage. — U.S. ed.
       p. cm. — (People & places)
    "A Templar book" — Verso of t.p.
    "First published in Great Britain in 1989 by Macmillan Children's
Books" — Verso of t.p.
    Includes index.
    Summary: Text and illustrations introduce the geography, history,
people, and culture of the countries of Central America.
    1. Central America—Juvenile literature. [1. Central America.]
I. Savage, Ann, ill. II. Title. III. Series: People & places
(Englewood Cliffs, N.J.)
F1428.5.M67   1989
972.8—dc 19   89-5855
ISBN 0-382-09824-2   CIP
                                   AC

Contents

WHERE IN THE WORLD?

Central America is the narrow neck of land, or isthmus, between North and South America. It is made up of the republics of Nicaragua, El Salvador, Costa Rica, Honduras, Panama, Guatemala, and Belize (formerly British Honduras). Although Panama belongs to Central America geographically, it is closer to South America in terms of its environment and history. Mexico, between the republics and the United States, is not considered to be part of Central America. Bay Islands (Islas de la Bahia) belong to Honduras.

The isthmus is bordered on the east by the Caribbean Sea, which is part of the Atlantic Ocean, and on the west by the Pacific Ocean. In places, the land is very narrow. In parts of Panama it is just 50 miles wide. This made possible the construction of the Panama Canal, which links the Atlantic and Pacific Oceans.

Today's population is made up of native Indians, the descendants of explorers and settlers from Europe, as well as the descendants of slaves from Africa and the West Indies. Spanish is the principal language.

Petén

The Petén is a jungle-covered tableland of about 13,460 square miles that extends through north Guatemala, Belize, and Mexico. It was the center of the great Maya civilization until around the 10th century. Since then it has been sparsely populated. Recently, however, settlers moving from the crowded cities have begun to explore the forests, and oil companies are searching for petroleum deposits.

Symbol of Central America

The quetzal has been described as the most beautiful bird in the world. It was worshiped by the Maya, the native people of Central America, who depicted it in their art. The quetzal is the national bird of Guatemala.

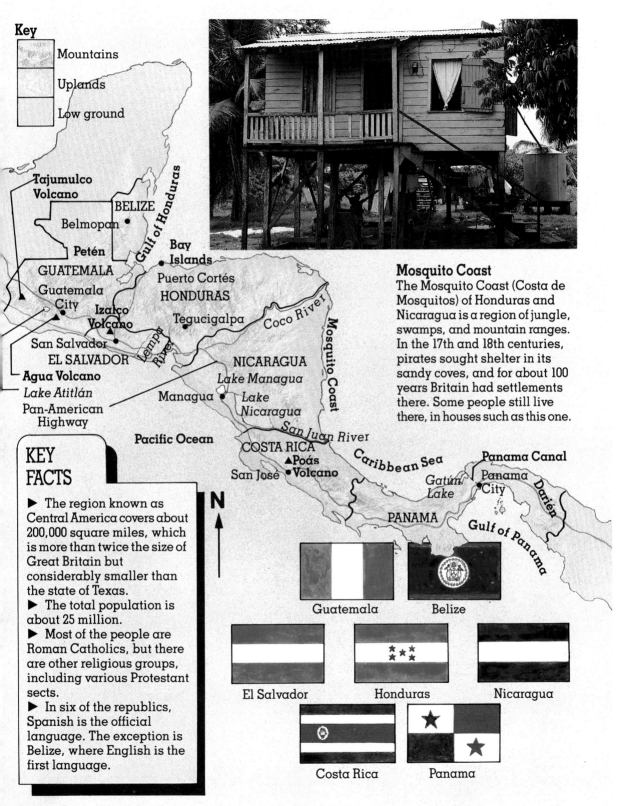

Key

- Mountains
- Uplands
- Low ground

Tajumulco Volcano

BELIZE

Belmopan •

Petén

GUATEMALA

Guatemala City

Izalco Volcano

San Salvador

EL SALVADOR

Agua Volcano

Lake Atitlán

Pan-American Highway

Gulf of Honduras

Bay Islands

Puerto Cortés

HONDURAS

Tegucigalpa •

Coco River

Mosquito Coast

NICARAGUA

Lake Managua

Managua • *Lake Nicaragua*

San Juan River

Pacific Ocean

COSTA RICA

San José • ▲Poás •Volcano

Caribbean Sea

Panama Canal

Gatún Lake

Panama City

Darién

PANAMA

Gulf of Panama

Mosquito Coast

The Mosquito Coast (Costa de Mosquitos) of Honduras and Nicaragua is a region of jungle, swamps, and mountain ranges. In the 17th and 18th centuries, pirates sought shelter in its sandy coves, and for about 100 years Britain had settlements there. Some people still live there, in houses such as this one.

KEY FACTS

► The region known as Central America covers about 200,000 square miles, which is more than twice the size of Great Britain but considerably smaller than the state of Texas.

► The total population is about 25 million.

► Most of the people are Roman Catholics, but there are other religious groups, including various Protestant sects.

► In six of the republics, Spanish is the official language. The exception is Belize, where English is the first language.

N

Guatemala   Belize

El Salvador   Honduras   Nicaragua

Costa Rica   Panama

LANDS OF VOLCANOES AND LAKES

All the republics of Central America lie within the area known as the Tropics. While the climate is hot and humid at sea level, the temperature changes according to altitude. There are no real seasons, only a difference in the amount of rainfall. From November to April is the driest part of the year.

Millions of years ago North and South America were not connected by land. The two great continents were separated by the sea. Movement of the great "plates" that lie beneath the earth's surface changed that. Sometime between 4 and 20 million years ago the Cocos and Caribbean plates came into contact. The clash thrust up the mountainous, volcanic Central America isthmus.

Volcanic eruptions and earthquakes in Central America have caused great disasters. Cities have been destroyed and thousands of people have died. The only positive outcome has been the buildup of volcanic ash, which has made the soil fertile.

Guatemala earthquakes and volcanoes
In 1773 the old capital of Guatemala, Antigua, was destroyed by the Agua Volcano. In Central America's greatest disaster in 1976, 20,000 people lost their lives and 200,000 dwellings were destroyed in an earthquake. Other earthquakes occurred in 1902, 1917, and 1918.

Lake Nicaragua
The largest freshwater lakes in Central America are in Nicaragua. Lake Nicaragua is more than 4,800 square miles, and Lake Managua is about 5,440 square miles. Because of its location, Lake Nicaragua has been considered as a possible site for another Pacific-Atlantic canal.

Volcano range

The line of volcanic mountains that runs from Guatemala south through El Salvador, Nicaragua, and Costa Rica to Panama is impressive. About 50 are said to be active. Others are dormant, though still capable of eruption. Here is Poás Volcano in Costa Rica.

Hurricanes

Hurricane Joan hit the Caribbean coast of Nicaragua and Honduras late in 1988. It devastated the town of Bluefields, killing at least 50 people and making 300,000 homeless.

KEY FACTS

▶ The highest volcano in Central America, Tajumulco, in Guatemala, is 13,845 feet high.

▶ Temperature zones in the mountains can be divided into *tierra caliente*, or hot land (sea level to 2,998 feet); *tierra templada*, or mild land (2,998 to 5,997 feet); and *tierra fría*, or cold land (5,997 feet upward).

▶ The heaviest rainfall is in northern Honduras and Guatemala. The yearly average is in excess of 79 inches (whereas Britain has less than 39 inches a year). On certain parts of the east and west coasts, twice as much rain falls on the Caribbean side as on the Pacific.

▶ El Salvador has the largest number of volcanoes on the isthmus, including Izalco. This volcano earned its name "Lighthouse of the Pacific" because at one time it was almost continuously active.

▶ Honduras is the only Central American country that does not have volcanoes.

A TROPICAL HOTHOUSE

The plant and animal life of Central America is very varied. Soil made fertile by volcanic ash and a tropical climate have created many forests. The area's location as a land bridge between North and South America makes the region unique, because wildlife from both continents live there. Tropical rainforest covers the gentle Caribbean slopes up to a height of about 2,998 feet. Its tall trees are supported by large roots and covered with vines, creepers, and other plants. The forest on the steeper, drier Pacific side has both deciduous and evergreen trees. In other areas there is cloud forest, where orchids and tree ferns grow, as well as coniferous forest, an alpine zone of low tough shrubs, and regions of dry cactus.

As in other parts of the world, great areas of forest are being cut down for commercial reasons. This causes problems for wildlife, whose homes are being destroyed. To counteract this, national parks and reserves have been created on different parts of the isthmus. Costa Rica and Nicaragua have recently agreed to a "peace park" in a disputed border area. It includes the largest virgin tropical rainforest on the isthmus.

An island laboratory
When the Panama Canal was built, Barro Colorado, an island covered with tropical forest, formed in one of the many lakes that form the Canal Zone. It became a haven for wildlife, with more than 1,000 species of plants and 250 species of birds. There has been a biological field laboratory there since 1923.

Pacific turtle

Saving the turtles
A number of rare marine turtles live on the Caribbean beaches of Central America. Turtles are killed for their eggs, meat, and their shells. A conservation program started in 1954 in Costa Rica is helping to save them from extinction.

10

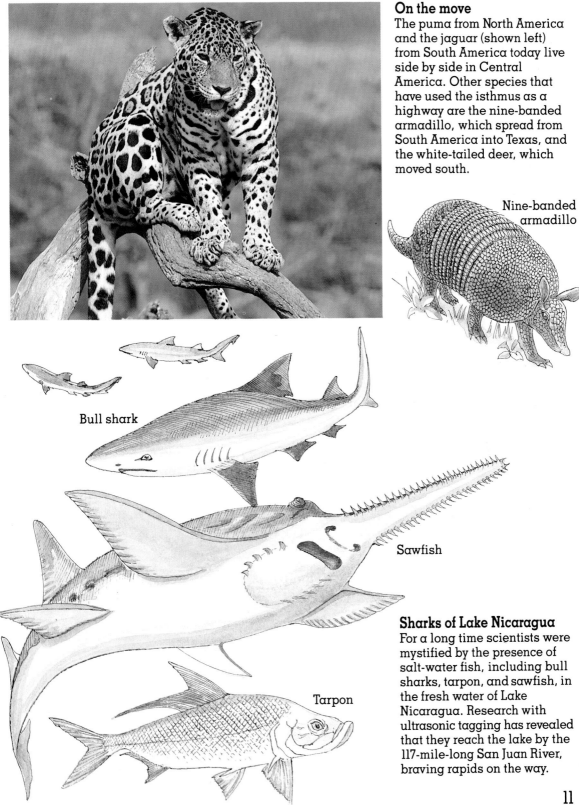

On the move

The puma from North America and the jaguar (shown left) from South America today live side by side in Central America. Other species that have used the isthmus as a highway are the nine-banded armadillo, which spread from South America into Texas, and the white-tailed deer, which moved south.

Nine-banded armadillo

Bull shark

Sawfish

Tarpon

Sharks of Lake Nicaragua

For a long time scientists were mystified by the presence of salt-water fish, including bull sharks, tarpon, and sawfish, in the fresh water of Lake Nicaragua. Research with ultrasonic tagging has revealed that they reach the lake by the 117-mile-long San Juan River, braving rapids on the way.

11

THE PEOPLE OF CENTRAL AMERICA

When Christopher Columbus first arrived in Central America in 1502, many tribes of people were living in the forests and mountains of the isthmus. The Spaniards who followed in Columbus' footsteps at the beginning of the 16th century called all the native peoples "Indians" in the mistaken belief that Columbus had reached the Indies. During the years that followed, the Spaniards fought the Indians. This was known as the Spanish Conquest. They brought disease with them, reducing the number of Indians dramatically. At the same time the Spaniards, few of whom had wives, married the local women. Their descendants are known as mestizo, or "mixed blood."

Other peoples who settled in Central America included blacks — African slaves and Black Caribs — and Chinese brought in to work on the railroads and plantations. Immigrants from other European countries than Spain arrived in the 19th century, substantially increasing the number of whites.

Mestizos, Indians, whites, and blacks live in all the Central American countries in varying proportions.

KEY FACTS

▶ The region is uniquely rich in Indian languages, with at least 25 still in use. The most widely spoken is Maya.
▶ El Salvador is the smallest and most densely populated country in Central America. It covers just 8,416 square miles and has a population of almost 5 million.
▶ Most people live in the highlands because the climate is more comfortable there. This is where most of the cities are located.
▶ Apart from the Maya, other Indian peoples that still survive include the Jicaques, Miskito, Payas (Honduras); Izalco and Panchos (El Salvador); Bribri and Cabecar (Costa Rica); the Guaymi, Choco, and Cuna (Panama).

Mestizos
In Central America as a whole, the majority of people are of mixed Spanish-Indian descent. They are known as mestizos. They dress in Western-style clothes, mostly work in the towns, and speak Spanish.

Cuna Indians

The Cuna Indians live on the San Blas Islands of Panama, where they live mainly by sea fishing. Other communities of Cuna live on the mainland. They farm, growing a variety of crops, and produce crafts, using wood to fashion many of the articles they need. They also weave and make baskets. Traditional dress includes gold nose rings, and garments decorated with colorful appliqués.

Black Caribs

Early in the 17th century some "free" black African slaves arrived on the island of St. Vincent in the Caribbean. They mixed with the local Carib population, thus producing "Black Caribs." In 1797 a group of Black Caribs was deported to Roatán, one of the Bay Islands off the coast of Honduras. From there some made their way to the mainland. Today their descendants make a living from fishing.

Costeños of Nicaragua

Nicaragua has been described as "two countries." This is because the people of the Atlantic coast, the costeños, are different from the Spanish descendants of the rest of the country. Many costeños are descended from slaves introduced by the British. They speak a form of English, are Protestants, and have a different culture.

13

THE ANCIENT MAYA CIVILIZATION

By far the greatest civilization in Central America before the Spanish Conquest was the Maya. It was at its height from about AD 300 to 900, when it was centered on the lowland, jungle-covered Petén area of Guatemala.

The Maya were advanced in the sciences and the arts. They built magnificent cities with huge stone temples and pyramids. Yet they had no knowledge of the wheel or metal tools. In the Americas of ancient times they were the only people with a system of writing. They also had remarkable knowledge of astronomy.

The Maya were advanced in agriculture — particularly in the cultivation of maize (corn) and beans — and farmed different areas of the forest in turn to prevent the soil from becoming thin through over-use. Worship of the gods — which included the jaguar, the feared king of the forest — was important, particularly to ensure good harvests. The Maya civilization was made up of a number of city-states that were constantly at war. The purpose of these wars was not just to gain land, but also to take captives who were then sacrificed.

Maya codexes
A codex was a sort of picture book — a series of sheets with picture writing. The Maya often used codexes to illustrate topics related to the calendar or festivals. Codexes also provide us with details of how the Maya society was organized.

Copán, Honduras
Copán, in present-day Honduras, was one of the southernmost Maya cities. The site was bought for $30 in 1839 by an American, John Lloyd Stephens. He was in the area with artist Frederick Catherwood, in order to record the remains of the ancient city. Intensive restoration work was carried out in the 1930s, when the Copán River had to be diverted to avoid further erosion of the buildings.

Tikal

Tikal, an important Maya city, covered an area of about 6 square miles in the rainforest of Guatemala's Petén. Among the surviving buildings is the Great Temple of the Jaguar, or Temple I, which was built in the 8th century and is over 16 feet high.

Mayan ball game

One of the main features at Copán is the ball court shown at the right. A ball game was played between two opposing teams using a very heavy rubber ball. Because it could be dangerous, players wore protective clothing. The game is thought to have had a religious meaning. It is the forerunner of many sports, such as football.

ARRIVAL OF THE SPANIARDS

Christopher Columbus reached the mainland of Central America on his fourth voyage in 1502. There were many rumors that the area contained gold and minerals, so explorers and soldiers followed him there. At first they concentrated their search for gold around Panama and in Mexico.

The conquest of Central America began with two Spanish captains. Hernán Cortés in Mexico sent his men south, and Pedro Arias de Avila in Panama sent his men north. The Spaniards were few in number, but because they were on horseback and carrying metal weapons, they were able to surprise and defeat the far more numerous tribes of Indians.

Only what is now Honduras proved to be rich in mineral resources: the capital, Tegucigalpa, is an Indian name meaning "silver hill." In most of Central America during the colonial period, settlements grew up around the plantations, forests, and cattle herds. Among products important for trade were cacao (cocoa beans), sugar, and the dyes cochineal and indigo.

The Spanish government imposed an administrative system headed by a viceroy. Missionaries and priests worked, sometimes in the remotest areas, to convert the people to the Catholic faith.

Cacao
Cacao (from which cocoa and chocolate are made) was highly prized in Central America under Spanish rule. The Spaniards believed that drinking chocolate gave them energy and cured illnesses.

Pirates
During the 17th and 18th centuries pirates often attacked Spanish ships as they sailed for Europe full of silver and gold taken from Central America. In 1670 the English pirate Henry Morgan stormed Panama City and carried off 195 mule loads of booty.

Henry Morgan

Antigua

Antigua, in Guatemala, was founded in 1543 and was the most splendid city in Central America before the 1773 earthquake. A center of government and learning, it had a population of 60,000, a university, a printing press, a fine cathedral (shown here), numerous churches, and a palace of the Captains General.

Bartolomé de las Casas

After the conquest, the Spaniards treated the Indians very badly. They either turned them into slaves or killed them. Only the Indians of Guatemala successfully retreated into the hills. One man who witnessed the savagery and protested to the Spanish crown was the Catholic priest Bartolomé de las Casas. His defense of the Indians during the 16th century led to the passage of new laws for their protection.

Lenca Lempira

The currency of Honduras is named after Lenca Lempira, 16th-century Indian chief. With his army of 30,000 Indians, he resisted a fierce Spanish attack. Later he was deceived by the Spanish captain Pedro de Alvarado, and killed. He became a national hero.

THE NEW REPUBLICS

By the beginning of the 19th century the New World colonies were eager to break away from Spanish rule. Independence was declared in 1821 in Guatemala. In 1824 a federation called the United States of Central America was created between Guatemala, Honduras, Nicaragua, El Salvador, and Costa Rica. An early attempt was made to abolish slavery and help the Indians, but the federation lasted only a few years. Panama remained a colony of Colombia in South America until 1903.

The federation crumbled because of fighting between the Conservatives, representing the rich landowners and the Church, and the Liberals, who wanted reforms. This struggle continued throughout the 19th century. In all the other countries except Costa Rica, where democratic government by the people was established, war, disorder, assassination, and rule by dictators were common.

As in colonial times, agricultural exports were the most important part of the economy, helped by the introduction of coffee and bananas to the republics. Better roads and railroads were built to transport produce to the ports. By the turn of the century, the plantations were run by large North American companies, but the profits went to only a few people. Life for the poorly paid remained much the same.

Francisco Morozan
Known as the "Defender of Central America," Francisco Morozan worked harder than any other person for the formation of a United States of Central America. He was the president of the federation in 1830, and later became president of Honduras.

Panama railroad
The railroad was constructed from Colón to Panama City to carry pioneers on their way from Europe to the gold rush in California. It took four years to build, with many lives lost, at a cost of $8 million. It was completed in 1855.

Banana republics

The nickname "banana republics" was given to the Central America republics because of the quantity of bananas they exported.

Canal attempt

Having successfully built the Suez Canal in Africa, which connects the Mediterranean and the Red Sea, the Frenchman Ferdinand-Marie de Lesseps arrived in Panama in 1881 to build a sea-level canal across the isthmus. One of his workmen in 1886 and 1887 was Paul Gauguin, the French painter. However, conditions were appalling, thousands died from disease, and de Lesseps' company was finally forced to give up the project.

DICTATORS AND DEMOCRACY

The need for change was clear in Central America from the early years of the 20th century. The people resented the dictators, the rich landowning classes, and increasingly the role of the United States in their countries. When U.S. Marines occupied Nicaragua from 1926 to 1933, a revolutionary leader, Augusto Cesar Sandino, formed a guerrilla army to fight against the U.S. presence. In El Salvador in 1932 there was an unsuccessful revolt by some workers against the men who owned the coffee plantations. In the 1950s in Guatemala, when the elected president Jacobo Arbenz tried to divide up the large estates owned by the wealthy, he was removed from office.

The United States, anxious for things to stay as they were in the region, generally backed whoever was in power. In particular it gave its support to the Somoza family in Nicaragua. The Somozas — a father and two sons — ruled Nicaragua harshly for almost 50 years, until they were overthrown in 1979 by the guerrilla group known as the "Sandinistas." In neighboring El Salvador and Guatemala, though both have recently elected governments, guerrilla forces continue to fight for change.

Archbishop Romero
For most of the 1980s El Salvador has been on the edge of a state of civil war. There have been thousands of deaths. One victim was the Archbishop of San Salvador, Monsignor Oscar Romero, who regularly spoke out against unfair conditions. He was assassinated while saying mass.

Football war
In 1969 violence against a large community of El Salvadorians illegally living in Honduras led to fighting between the two countries. This bad feeling coincided with the qualifying game for the 1970 World Cup and sparked off the so-called "football war." It lasted for several days and more than 2,000 people were killed.

20

Contras

After the Sandinistas gained control in Nicaragua, relations with the United States worsened. In 1981 President Reagan authorized financial support for the Contras (their name means "those against") in their guerrilla war against the Sandinistas. However, opposition to the policy has now forced the U.S. government to drop this support. Here, two contra instructors take part in a training class for troops.

Anastasio Somoza Garcia

Father of the Somoza family, he took power in 1936 and was dictator for 19 years. He became Nicaragua's largest landowner and coffee producer and the richest person in Central America. He was assassinated in 1956 by a young poet.

Alliance for Progress

In the early 1960s President John F. Kennedy introduced the Alliance for Progress program. This program was designed to give financial and technical assistance to all Central and South American countries to help improve standards of living. Aid workers were involved in medical, educational, and social projects. Funds were spent on useful equipment like the tractor above.

THE COUNTRY OF FRIENDSHIP

The history of Costa Rica has been quite different from that of the other republics since independence and the breakup of the Federation of the United States of Central America in 1838. This tiny nation has enjoyed peace, prosperity, and democracy. A constitution adopted in 1871 lasted until 1949. In 1890 the first free and honest presidential election of Central America took place, and universal suffrage (votes for all adults) was introduced in 1913. A tradition of orderly government has existed ever since. Costa Rica has kept itself apart from the troubles of its neighbors. It showed that it was determined to keep its peaceful position by getting rid of its army in 1948.

Unlike the rest of Central America, Costa Rica's population is mostly Spanish, and on average the people enjoy the highest standard of living in the region. The economy is based on agricultural produce. However, in recent years it has been in trouble with rising inflation and unemployment, strikes, and an increasing foreign debt. Successful measures introduced by President Monge between 1982 and 1986 have lessened these problems.

Costa Rica stones
Stone spheres like this one, which are almost perfectly round, are found scattered throughout the countryside. Their age and purpose remain a mystery.

San José
Founded in 1737, San José is the capital of Costa Rica. It is situated in a broad, fertile valley almost in the center of the country, at an altitude of 3,770 feet. Over a million people — more than one-third of the country's population — live there.

Coco Island

Costa Rica owns the tiny, uninhabited Coco Island, 370 miles off the Pacific coast. Seventeenth-century pirates are said to have buried treasure looted from Spanish ships there.

Guanacaste

Guanacaste is sometimes referred to as the "brown" province of Costa Rica. This is because most people are of a Spanish-Indian-African mix, and it is cattle country. Cowboys dressed in leather and wearing wide-brimmed hats drive the herds across the land by day, and enjoy evenings of impromptu music and dancing.

Ox carts

Colorful, hand-painted ox carts were once used to transport coffee to the ports. A few of these are still in use today.

KEY FACTS

▶ Costa Rica was the first country in Central America to cultivate coffee.

▶ It is the second smallest of the republics, divided into seven provinces. Its population is two and a half million.

▶ Costa Rica has four volcanoes. Two — Irazú and Poás — are still active. Its highest mountain peak is Chirripó, 12,530 feet high.

▶ Puerto Limon, on the Caribbean coast, is the main port. It handles more than two million "hands," or bunches, of bananas each year.

▶ The president and members of the Legislative Assembly are elected every four years. Everyone over 18 has the right to vote.

▶ The people of Costa Rica are called "Ticos."

BELIZE

Belize was formerly known as British Honduras, and was the last British colony on the American mainland. It became independent in 1981 and is a member of the British Commonwealth.

The colony began as a settlement on the Belize River in 1638 when the Spaniards allowed British settlers to cut trees for wood. The British settlement prospered and by the end of the 18th century was strong enough to defend itself from several attacks by the Spaniards. In 1862 the British government appointed a governor, and in 1871 British Honduras was declared a crown colony. This meant that it belonged to Britain. The newly independent Spanish colonies were worried about the British presence; and a dispute with Guatemala, which have always claimed Belize as its own, has never been settled.

Belize has mountains, swamps, and jungles, and much forest. Timber products are still important to the economy, and *chicle*, a gum from the sapodilla tree, is used to make chewing gum. Although only a small proportion of the land is used for cultivation, sugar and citrus fruits are the major exports.

Mennonites
In 1958 some members of the Mennonite religious sect arrived from Mexico and settled in communities along the Belize River. They produce fresh milk and cheese and have introduced large-scale chicken farming.

Belmopan
The capital of the country was moved from Belize City to Belmopan in 1970. Belmopan mainly consists of administrative buildings.

Coral reef and islands

About 15 miles off the coast of Belize is the world's second largest barrier reef, about 199 miles long. It is fringed by many small islands known as cays, inhabited by fishermen.

The reef has some of the finest tropical marine fish in the Caribbean.

KEY FACTS

▶ Belize became independent on September 21, 1981.
▶ Victoria Peak, at 3,681 feet, is the highest point in Belize.
▶ Everyone over 18 has the right to vote. Elections normally take place every five years.
▶ There is a national assembly of an elected house of representatives, and a senate appointed by the governor-general. The governor-general, representing the British crown, appoints a prime minister and an opposition leader from the house of representatives.
▶ The only railroad in Belize is a line for carrying logs.
▶ The population of Belize is 170,000 with over 50 percent of mixed origin. The rest are European, North American, Maya Indian, and Black Carib.
▶ The British keep a military force of about 1,500 men in Belize.

George Price

George Price, the country's first prime minister, was the politician most responsible for achieving independence in Belize. He leads the People's United Party (PUP).

RICHES FROM THE SOIL AND SEA

A griculture is the most important part of the Central American economy. Coffee, bananas, cotton, corn, sugar, cocoa, tobacco, and rice are grown in all the Central American republics.

The North American United Fruit Company began trading in bananas before the end of the last century. Most of its plantations were on the hot, humid Caribbean coast. It was immediately successful. When disease threatened to destroy the east coast crop, the company had to move some of its operations to the Pacific coast, where the harvest proved even better. Occasionally other hazards threaten production of bananas and in 1974 Hurricane Fifi destroyed nearly all the Honduran crop.

Like most developing countries, the Central American republics rely heavily on one or two crops, such as coffee and bananas, for their export market. A sudden drop in the world price for any of these particular crops could have a devastating effect on the local economy.

Still another problem in Central America is the ownership of large areas of land by relatively few people. Several countries are trying to introduce reform to break up the big estates.

Bananas
Bananas take about nine months to grow to a bunch weighing about 118 pounds. They are cut into smaller bunches called "hands," then washed, boxed, and shipped within 48 hours of being picked.

Coffee
Coffee is the leading commercial crop for the export market. Coffee is made from the beanlike seeds of a tall tropical shrub. Shown here are ripening coffee beans.

Shrimp fishing

In Panama, fishing, particularly for deep-sea shrimps, has increased in importance. Panama is now ranked as the world's third largest exporter of shrimps.

Cattle industry

Cattle are raised for beef, milk, and hides. Much of the beef is exported to the United States. The most common cattle breed is the Zebu, although some European and American breeds are also popular.

DEVELOPING INDUSTRY

E l Salvador and Guatemala are the most industrialized Central American countries. The main industries include textiles, drugs for medicines, and machinery. Other industries, such as food and fish processing, are related to agriculture and trade in leather and hides. Computer components, automobile parts, and electrical appliances are made for export.

Central America has some mineral resources, among them gold, silver, manganese, mercury, iron, lead, and tin. Deposits of copper have been found in Panama. In Costa Rica a recent discovery of bauxite, used in making aluminum, has led to large-scale investment in a plant to produce aluminum. Some oil deposits have been found, notably in Guatemala, but most petroleum is imported. Large-scale hydroelectric projects are underway in several countries. In Nicaragua and Guatemala wood is widely used as fuel.

However, industrial development in the region is slow because the unstable political situation discourages people investing in local industry.

Puerto Cortés
The Spanish explorer and captain Hernan Cortés founded the city of Puerto Cortés in Honduras. With its deep harbor, it is now one of the most important and modern ports on the Atlantic coast.

Hydroelectricity
In the past 30 years many hydroelectric dams have been built, particularly in El Salvador and Costa Rica.

Timber

Central America has a small timber industry. In addition to mahogany, which has been traded for many years, the forests contain other valuable woods, such as cedar, pine, oak, teak, and balsa.

Tourism

The tourist industry has remained small, but visitors who make the journey can enjoy spectacular scenery such as Lake Atitlán in Guatemala's Sierra Madre mountains.

CROSSING THE ISTHMUS

When the Frenchman de Lesseps failed in his attempt to build a canal across the isthmus, the United States took up the challenge. In 1903 a treaty was signed giving the United States control over an area 10 miles wide and 40 miles in length coast to coast between the Atlantic and Pacific oceans. This area was called the Pacific Canal Zone.

Engineers constructed the 51-mile-long zigzag Panama Canal within the zone. They had to work under very bad conditions, and were plagued by disease. The canal was completed in 1914. Particularly difficult was Gaillard Cut, a channel carved out of nearly 8 miles of solid rock. Named after the engineer in charge of the digging, it still has to be constantly dredged to keep it clear of earth slides.

As a result of growing opposition to the role of the United States in Panama, the U.S. government has agreed to let Panama have control of the canal and the Canal Zone by the end of this century.

William C. Gorgas
Many thousands of workers building the canal died from yellow fever and malaria. Conditions only improved when Colonel Gorgas discovered ways of controlling the diseases. It is believed that he is responsible for freeing the region of yellow fever.

Pan-American Highway
The paved Pan-American Highway runs the length of Central America. It forms an almost continuous road link between North and South America, except for the Darién region of Panama. There are plans to build a road through the Darién Gap. But for the moment only adventurous travelers or explorers make the hazardous journey overland from Panama to Colombia through the rough jungle.

The Panama Canal

Ships sailing from the Atlantic to the Pacific exit the canal 27 miles to the east of where they entered.

Lock system

There is a difference of about 85 feet in altitude between the two oceans and the central part of the isthmus. To allow for this, the engineers created a system of locks, in which the level of the water can be controlled. Ships are pulled through the locks by small engines that run alongside on tracks.

By train

Nicaragua's government helps pay for running the country's trains, so everyone can afford to use them. Overcrowding is very common.

LIVING, WORKING, AND EATING

Traditionally the people of Central America have lived in the country, but in recent years many people have moved to the cities and towns, hoping for a better way of life. Most city dwellers, working in government offices, banks, and other professional occupations, have televisions, cars, and other consumer goods. The best schools and hospitals are in the towns, where there is adequate electricity and sanitation. Unfortunately, however, the people arriving from the countryside often have difficulty finding work. Many have to live in shanty towns, making a living as best they can.

Life outside the towns is difficult for the small farmers in the highlands and the plantation workers on the coast. Home is probably a mud-brick or wooden clapboard house, often without any modern conveniences. To earn extra income, many families make traditional handicrafts, to sell in local markets. Or they work in shops or as taxi drivers.

Role of women
Many women were actively involved in the Sandinista revolution in Nicaragua. They later formed their own organizations, and have since taken an active part in reshaping the country after the fall of the Somozas. They have done much work in education, helping people to learn to read and write, and have helped to improve living conditions.

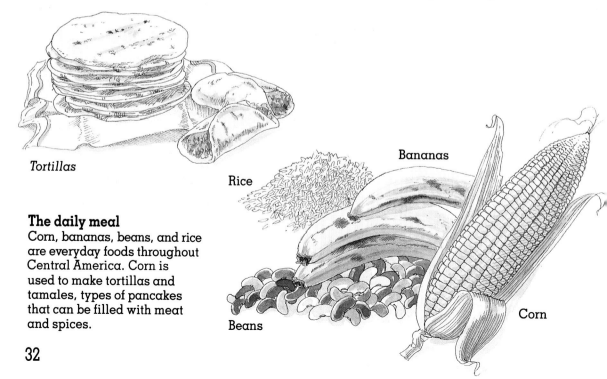

Tortillas

Rice

Bananas

Corn

Beans

The daily meal
Corn, bananas, beans, and rice are everyday foods throughout Central America. Corn is used to make tortillas and tamales, types of pancakes that can be filled with meat and spices.

Housing

The designs and building materials of houses in Central American countries are chosen to suit the areas they are in. For example, in the highlands there are adobe (mud) brick houses. On the coast, clapboard (wooden board) houses are often built on stilts. In the lower areas, one-story houses are made of bamboo and dried sugar cane. In the forest, Indians use palm thatch. In the cities there are fine colonial and modern brick-built dwellings.

THE INDIANS OF GUATEMALA

I n Guatemala almost half the population of eight million is Indian, descendants of the Maya. Their traditional way of life is largely independent of the rest of the country. They have their own style of dress, speak their own Indian languages, and practice their own form of worship. They mostly live in communities in the highland plains, around Chichicastenango and Lake Atitlán.

Some Indians are employed as seasonal labor on big farms, but mostly they earn a living by farming small plots of land. There they grow corn, beans, and squash. On land near Lake Atitlán they plant some European crops, such as onions, cabbages, and carrots. Surplus food and some handicrafts are traded at local markets for cash. Land is traditionally passed from father to son. However, if there is not enough land to do this, some members of the family have to seek work in the mestizo society. The Maya who adopt Western dress and customs are known as *ladinos*. They are often not welcomed back into their villages.

Handicrafts
The Maya have inherited the skills of their ancestors in weaving and embroidery. Today they sell many items to tourists, such as hats, napkins, baskets, pottery, and woven garments.

Dress
The Guatemalan Indian women wear ankle-length, richly patterned skirts, tunics, and headdresses. The men, too, dress colorfully, with decorative sashes, kerchiefs, hatbands, and tassels. Their clothing has not changed much since the Spaniards arrived in their country 400 years ago.

Markets

The market is more than just a place to buy and sell produce. It is also a meeting place, where Indians gather to socialize.

Fiestas

Fiestas are celebrations that combine Christian ritual with traditional beliefs. The Indians honor many gods, particularly those they believe can bring good harvests.

FAMILY LIFE

T he family is very important at all levels of society in Central America. It has been made stronger by extending the family to include *compadres*, similar to godparents. Several generations often live in the same house, and no matter how little money the family has, occasions such as confirmation and marriage are celebrated in traditional style.

War and civil strife have brought much hardship to family life. In Nicaragua, after the 1979 revolution, about one-fifth of the population was homeless. Other problems include lack of proper food, a high birthrate, and short life expectancy. In many parts of Central America, medical facilities are inadequate, and there is a shortage of doctors, nurses, and equipment. International agencies, such as the World Health Organization, help families wherever possible. However, such basic problems as providing clean drinking water have yet to be overcome in many places.

Family fun
This fair is in El Salvador. Families in Central America like to have a day out together, and children enjoy visiting the fair.

After the revolution
Before the Nicaraguan revolution this house was the home of a farm manager. Now it has been converted into a nursery for children of the families that live and work on the farm.

Health care
Costa Rica has better medical facilities than the other republics. There are good hospitals and clinics and everyone can receive free medical attention. Costa Rica also has a Red Cross Society.

Religion
Most of the population of Central America is Roman Catholic. The people attend church regularly and celebrate Christian festivals, in particular Holy Week at Easter and Christmas. Many people consider the most important religious event to be the annual fiesta to the patron saint of their village.

LEARNING AND LISTENING

Preschool, primary, secondary, and university education are available in all the republics. They are free everywhere, but many children do not go to school. This may be because they need to work to help their families or because, as in Nicaragua, there are not enough schools available. Schools are run by the governments or the Church. Some are private. A few plantation owners provide schools for the workers' children.

Educational facilities are much better in the towns than in rural districts. In Guatemala there is a particular problem in providing schooling for the Indians, who often do not speak Spanish. Universities and technical colleges are found in most of the major cities.

Plans to use radio for educational purposes are already underway. Radio is popular and makes it possible to communicate, particularly with communities living in the remotest areas of the isthmus. So few people own television sets that its use for educational purposes is still limited.

KEY FACTS

▶ Costa Rica, where more people can read and write than in any other Latin American country, spends almost one-third of the national budget on education.
▶ The oldest university in Central America is San Carlos de Guatemala. It was founded in Guatemala City in 1676.
▶ All the republics produce their own newspapers.
▶ Figures from 1981 show that fewer than 80 students per 1,000 reach higher education in Guatemala, Honduras, Nicaragua, and El Salvador.

Selling newspapers
Newspapers and magazines are sold from stands on street corners and by street sellers. Sometimes foreign magazines can be bought. Press censorship has existed in a number of the republics at different times.

Nicaragua's National Literacy Campaign

In 1979, at the time of Nicaragua's revolution, more than half the population could not read or write. A literacy campaign was launched, directed by Father Fernando Cardenal. It was supported by newly trained teachers, specially published books, and thousands of young people, over half of them women, who volunteered to help in rural communities. The illiteracy rate was reduced from 50.3 percent to 12.9 percent in just a few months.

Out to work

Instead of going to school, some children work to help provide money for the family. In the cities they sell fruit and refreshments, wash cars, clean shoes, or run errands. In the country they work on the farms.

THE CULTURAL LIFE

The Maya civilization and centuries of Spanish rule have left a rich history of culture in Central America. Ancient sites like Tikal and Copán are well known, but other palaces and temples still lie hidden in the dense forests. There are also many colonial churches with gold altars and decorated facades, and fine buildings in cities like Antigua in Guatemala, and Comayagua, the former capital of Honduras.

Indian and Spanish traditions are still strong in the republics. These influences are reflected in the literature and art of the region, in music and musical instruments, dances, festivals, and handicrafts. To promote the arts, most countries have national libraries, institutes of culture, and museums.

The developing film and television industry shows North American influence. Flourishing film companies in nearby Mexico and Cuba also have helped to make the cinema popular.

Miguel Angel Asturias
This Guatemalan novelist, who died in 1974, was awarded the Nobel Prize in 1967. His best known novel was *El Señor Presidente* (*The President*).

Ruben Dario
Nicaragua's famous poet Ruben Dario (1867-1916) had an important influence on Latin American literature. He created a new form of poetry called *modernismo*.

Political murals

The fire station in Léon, Nicaragua, is decorated with wall paintings, or murals. On the left, national hero Sandino has his foot on the head of Anastasio Somoza.

Crafts

Local artists produce a variety of crafts in Honduras, including weaving, woodcarvings, ceramics, macramé (cord knotted in designs), bead necklaces, and leather work.

HAVING FUN

Soccer and baseball are the favorite sports of Central Americans. They are watched by crowds in large city stadiums, and played by children in bare feet on pieces of scrub land in the countryside. These are sports that everyone can enjoy. Organized games, such as tennis and golf, are often played only in private clubs. Panama has produced world-class boxers. Wrestling is also popular.

The land of Central America is ideal for outdoor activities — walking and hiking in the highlands, exploring dense forests, and taking part in water sports on the coast. Some of the best swimming and snorkeling is around the Bay Islands. Most cities have parks where families and friends stroll and picnic.

Music and dancing are an important part of Central American life. All kinds of music are popular, from traditional Caribbean and Afro rhythms to waltzes and modern rock.

Marimbas
Bands playing marimbas are very popular. The instrument was introduced by African slaves. The keys are made from selected woods and played with small mallets.

Baseball in Managua
This baseball match is being played in the National Stadium, which holds 50,000. The game first became popular in Nicaragua when the U.S. military occupied the country from 1912. *Beis*, as it is called, is now enjoyed by many people.

42

Carnival time

There are many public holidays and festivals when the streets are turned into a riot of noise, color, and fun. Crowds of people in colorful carnival costumes take part, and there are processions, fireworks, and masked dancers.

Horse racing

Horse racing is popular in Panama. Races take place every weekend at the President Remon Track.

TOMORROW'S CENTRAL AMERICA

The Sandinista Revolution in Nicaragua in 1979 was very important in the history of Central America. For the first time people successfully fought against the old system of dictators and wealthy landowners. In El Salvador and Guatemala a similar struggle is taking place, with reports of assassination and bloodshed.

Many of the people of Central America want a greater say in their future and a fairer share of their countries' wealth. There are also people who would like to see change, but believe it can be achieved by negotiation. The best hope so far has come from a number of Central and South American countries that formed the Contadora group, so-called because their first meeting in 1983 took place on Contadora Island in Panama. They have suggested gradually reducing the supply and use of arms, and stopping interference from foreign countries. Its ideas have been widely welcomed.

President Arias
In 1987 President Arias of Costa Rica proposed a peace plan for Central America. This gained international support and he was awarded the Nobel Prize. The aim of the plan was to stop the civil wars in the region, to work toward democracy, and to set up a Central American parliament.

Adults of tomorrow
These children are from Chichicastenango in Guatemala.

44

Looking ahead
Most of the countries of Central America have had a stormy history. There has been political conflict and many natural disasters. Central Americans are hoping that the 21st century will bring a more peaceful future.

Future for the young
It is estimated that half the population of Nicaragua is under 20 years of age. Many young people were involved with the revolution and are now helping to rebuild their country. The key to a better future in Central America lies in their hands.

Index

Acknowledgments

All illustrations by Ann Savage.

Photographic credits (a = above, b = below, m = middle, l = left, r = right): Cover al South American Pictures, bl South American Pictures, ar Hutchison Library, br South American Pictures; page 7 Boutin/Zefa; page 8 Hallam Murray/South American Pictures (SAP); page 9 Peter Ryley/SAP; page 10 J.G. Fuller/Hutchison Library; page 11 Marion Morrison/SAP; page 13 Hilary Bradt/SAP; page 15 Flora Bottomley/SAP; page 16 Tony Morrison/SAP; page 17 Flora Bottomley/SAP; page 18 Robert Harding Picture Library; page 19 Hutchison Library; page 21 a Popperfoto, b J. Allan Cash Ltd; page 22 a Jevan Berrange/SAP, b MMichael Cannon/SAP; page 23 Peter Ryley/SAP; page 25 Robert Harding Picture Library; page 26 a Marion Morrison/SAP, b Edward Parker/SAP; page 27 Dr Nigel Smith/Hutchison Library; page 28 Rex Features; page 29 Flora Bottomley/SAP; page 30 Jevan Berrange/SAP; page 31 a Marion Morrison/SAP, b Gary Willis/SAP; page 33 a J.G. Fuller/Hutchison Library, m Charlotte Lipson/SAP, b Jevan Berrange/SAP; page 34 Hallam Murray/SAP; page 35 a Flora Bottomley/SAP, b Michael Macintyre/Hutchison Library; page 36 a Hallam Murray/SAP, b Gary Willis/SAP; page 37 Brian Moser/SAP; page 38 DAS Photo; page 39 Robert Harding Picture Library; page 41 Gary Willis/SAP; page 42 Gary Willis/SAP; page 43 Hilary Bradt/SAP; page 44 Hallam Murray/SAP; page 45 a Hallam Murray/SAP, b Gary Willis/SAP.